THIS BOOK BELONGS TO:

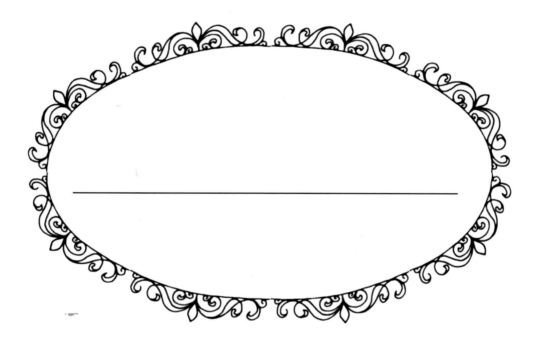

_____

GUTSY GIRL

D1225306

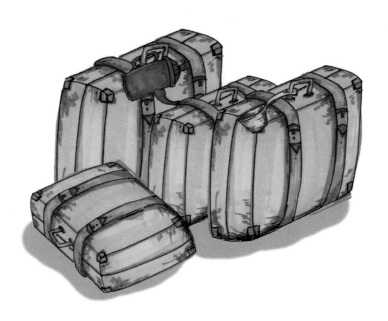

gutsy \guht-see\ adjective: brave, courageous, daring.

Showing determination even when your heart beats fast, your hands grow sweaty, and you fear failure.

Dedications

With oceans of gratitude to the gutsy women who line my life: Candace Catherine, Nancy Sue, Sara Renee, and Sarah Rose. —A.L.S.

Dedicated to my children: Melodee, Abraham, Jaden, and Eleanor. I love you! —B.A.W.

Gutsy Girls: Strong Christian Women Who Impacted the World
Book One: Gladys Aylward

All Rights Reserved © 2015 Amy L. Sullivan

Illustrations © 2015 Beverly A. Wines

ISBN-13: 978-0692518533

ISBN-10: 0692518533

Printed in the United States of America

Gutsy Girls

Strong Christian Women Who Impacted the World

Book One:
Gladys Aylward

Amy L. Sullivan
Illustrated by Beverly Ann Wines

Gladys Aylward was *not* extraordinary. In fact, Gladys Aylward was just plain ordinary.

While the average woman today stands 5'5" tall, Gladys barely reached 5'0". While others knew much about well-known books and faraway cultures, Gladys failed out of missionary school.

While some women's jobs included filing and teaching and treating patients, Gladys' only skills were those she learned working as a parlormaid and housekeeper: sweeping and dusting and clearing tea.

When people looked at Gladys Aylward, they didn't see anything special.

Instead, they saw average.

Plain.

Ordinary.

But ordinary Gladys had an extraordinary idea. She dreamed of telling the people of China about Jesus.

"China is too far away!"

"You can't speak Chinese!"

"How weak and foolish you are!"

Gladys ignored these words.

After two years of saving, Gladys bought a ticket for the Trans-Siberian Railroad. Traveling to China alone was dangerous. To make matters worse, a war was raging.

"You won't make it to China alive!"

"This is ridiculous!"

"That's not what ordinary girls do!"

Gladys packed her bags anyway.

Gladys gathered two suitcases: one for food (meat cubes, hardboiled eggs, baked beans, biscuits, and tea) and one for clothing (shirts, skirts, sweaters, and shoes). Gladys collected two pounds and nine pence (which equaled less than $10.00), her ticket, a passport, a fountain pen, and a Bible. Then Gladys tied a teakettle and a pan to the handles of two suitcases, and off she went!

For the first part of her trip to China, Gladys hopped on a train. Then she took a ship followed by another train.

Finally, Gladys boarded the Trans-Siberian Railroad.

The Trans-Siberian Railroad
chugged
through
Russia.

One night, when the train could go no further, Gladys slept on a snowy
railroad track surrounded by howling wolves.

"I hope I don't freeze in the Russian wilderness."

"Maybe this trip is too dangerous."

"I am sick of eating meat cubes and hardboiled eggs!"

But Gladys pushed on.

Gladys continued her travels by boat, train, and bus. She crossed three mountain ranges, and for the last part of her journey, a mule carried her along steep mountain paths.

When Gladys finally arrived in Yangchen, China, the people did not trust her. In fact, some even threw mud at her and called Gladys names.

"Why are you here, foreign devil?"

"What could you do to help us?"

"You can keep your stories of Jesus!"

Gladys continued on.

In China, Gladys met another English woman. Together they opened the Inn of Eight Happinesses where they served weary travelers. The women fed their guests both food and stories of Jesus.

At this time in China, orphan children were bought and sold as slaves. Gladys found out and began to rescue children by taking them into the inn and adopting them, letting them fill the air with happy sounds of play.

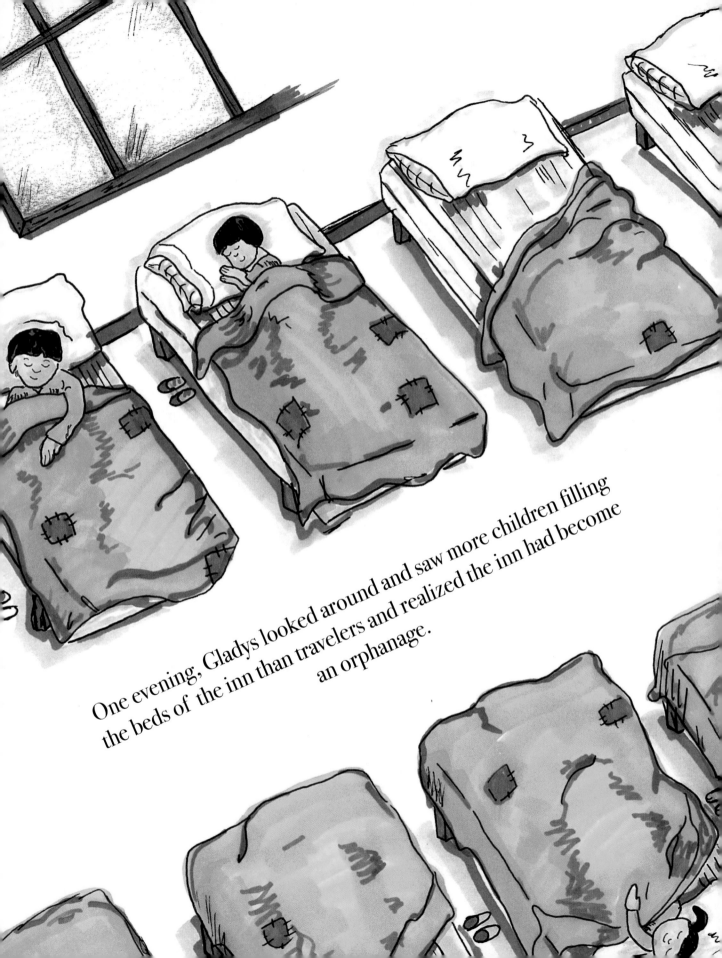

One evening, Gladys looked around and saw more children filling the beds of the inn than travelers and realized the inn had become an orphanage.

Gladys also found other ways to serve the people of China. She helped calm a riot in a local prison.

"Stop it! Tell me why you are fighting like this!" Gladys demanded.

Gladys became a foot inspector
and taught people why they shouldn't
bind the feet of children.

"Unwrap the feet of these girls! How can this poor
child walk with her feet bound up?"

Years passed, and slowly the people of China started to accept Gladys.

"Maybe she does really care about us."

"Maybe there is something to this God of hers."

"Maybe we should call her Ai-weh-deh, *Virtuous One*."

When war broke out in China, Gladys worked as a spy. Tiny Gladys hid from Japanese soldiers among the wheat fields, crawled through mud, and dodged bullets. Gladys knew the people and mountains well, and no one suspected an ordinary woman capable of such bravery. Gladys discovered secrets about the enemy and reported back to Chinese soldiers.

When the dangers of war threatened the children at her inn, Gladys gathered 100 children and walked them over 100 miles through the mountains to safety. Along the way, they had little to eat and nowhere to sleep. They spent the night in caves and sometimes under nothing except the

dark,

black

sky.

Finally, after twenty-seven days, Gladys and the children arrived at their destination, and Gladys collapsed from exhaustion and sickness.

"How did you get the children across the mountain?"

"What did you and the children eat during those long twenty-seven days?"

"How strong and brave you are!"

Gladys showed the world that you don't have to be . . .

tall,

or smart,

or educated to serve.

Gladys showed us even ordinary people can be extraordinary for God.

That's gutsy.

Words for Gutsy Girls

1. **missionary** - a person sent by God to tell people about Jesus.

2. **binding feet** - an ancient Chinese custom in which ribbons were tied around young girls' feet to break them. This was very painful, and it kept girls from walking correctly. The binding of feet isn't practiced today.

3. **Ai-weh-deh** - Virtuous One (virtuous means good and honorable).

Historical Note

Because Gladys Aylward's life was full of adventure, her story may seem like fiction, but Gladys Aylward is not a fictional character. Her story is true. Gladys was a real-life missionary who served God by serving people.

Born in London, England, in 1902, Gladys loved to talk and act. As a child, she often imagined herself performing on stage. However, after attending a prayer meeting, Gladys decided she didn't want to spend her life acting, but instead, she wanted to live for God.

After reading an article about China in a magazine, Gladys realized millions of Chinese people had never heard of Jesus. Gladys tried to talk her Christian friends into going to China to tell people about Jesus, but they weren't interested. Gladys even encouraged her brother to travel to China to share God's Word to which he replied, "Not me! Why don't you go yourself?"

And so she did.

A Note From the Author

Dear Reader (Gutsy Girl),

Lean in. I want to tell you a secret.

Growing up, I wasn't gutsy.

When I was your age, I knew girls could do great things, but I thought great-thing-doers were the girls who won ribbons on Field Day and mastered multiplication facts in minutes. I was too tall and too shy to win any ribbons on Field Day, and mastering multiplication facts took work.

Can you relate?

At the time, I had no idea God loves the girls who don't win the race and get straight A's as much as He loves the girls who do.

It's true. God celebrates ordinary as much as He celebrates extraordinary.

Don't believe me?

The Bible is full of examples of God using people like Gladys Aylward who weren't extraordinary. God used lots of people who were just plain ordinary!

Who were these ordinary people God used?

I'm glad you asked.

- Peter, a simple fisherman, said he didn't know God three times, and God still made him a leader (Matthew 26:69-75).
- David, the youngest and smallest of Jesse's sons, was placed by God as the ruler of His people (I Samuel 16:7-12).
- Mary, a poor, teenage girl from a small town, became the mother of Jesus (Luke 1:28-33).

And this is only the beginning!

So, Gutsy Girl (yes, that's you!), embrace ordinary, and be brave. God created you perfectly perfect (completely and utterly ordinary) yet ready to serve Him in extraordinary ways.

Much Love,

Amy

Gutsy Girls
Strong Christian Women Who Impacted the World

Book One: Gladys Aylward

Book Two: Sisters Corrie and Betsie ten Boom

Book Three: Fanny Crosby

Book Four: Dr. Jennifer Wiseman

Book Five: Sojourner Truth

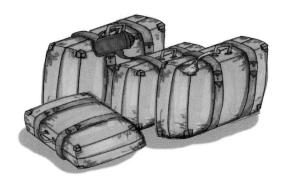

Sources

Aylward, Gladys and Hunter, Christine. *Gladys Aylward: The Little Woman* (Chicago, Illinois: Moody Publishers, 1970).

Benge, Geoff and Janet. *Gladys Aylward: The Adventure of a Lifetime* (Seattle, Washington, YWAM Publishing, 1998).

Brugess, Allen. *The Small Woman* (Cutchogue, New York: Buccaneer Books, 1996).

For free educational materials for classrooms, churches, and families, visit the author's website AmyLSullivan.com.

About the Author, Amy L. Sullivan

Amy L. Sullivan doesn't always feel brave, but her picture book series, *Gutsy Girls: Strong Christian Women Who Impacted the World*, allows her to comb through history and steal wisdom from the great women who came before her. Amy lives with her handsome husband, two daughters, naughty dog, and lazy cat in the mountains of Western North Carolina. Connect with Amy at AmyLSullivan.com.

About the Illustrator, Beverly Ann Wines

Beverly Ann Wines is an illustrator, painter, and art teacher. Beverly's art reflects who she is and what she loves. Beverly's art can be found in bookstores, homes, and galleries across the nation. You can learn more about Beverly's work by emailing her at Bvrlywines@aol.com or visiting her website Beverlysartandsoul.weebly.com.

Made in the USA
Middletown, DE
30 March 2019